Alphabetical Frolic

Alphabetical Frolic

Verse Pictures of Our Twenty-Six Scamps and Saints

RAYMOND H. HAAN

Illustrated by Chris M. Cook

RESOURCE *Publications* · Eugene, Oregon

ALPHABETICAL FROLIC
Verse Pictures of Our Twenty-Six Scamps and Saints

Resource Publications
An Imprint of Wipf and Stock Publishers
199 W. 8th Ave., Suite 3
Eugene, OR 97401

www.wipfandstock.com

PAPERBACK ISBN: 978-1-7252-7849-3
HARDCOVER ISBN: 978-1-7252-7848-6
EBOOK ISBN: 978-1-7252-7850-9

Manufactured in the U.S.A.   07/10/20

Dedicated
to
RONALD J. KOOISTRA,
whose wisdom knows
the value of wit,
and whose generous friendship
has always shared both

Acknowledgement

Any errors of word or judgment in this little volume exist only because I have been negligent in following the sharp-eyed and keen-minded counsel of *Kathleen Herrema*, indispensable critic, monitor, and advisor.

Introduction

No one needs to be told that the world is fickle and unstable as a daddy rabbit. Dependability and order are unpredictable, at best. A comfort it is, then, to contemplate the stability and orderliness of our beloved alphabet. Never do its twenty-six letters disappoint us: they have not disappeared or changed within our lifetimes—or during the lifetimes of our ancestors for hundreds of years. In fact, they have scarcely changed since ancient Roman times. Moreover, they pass their centuries in contentment, awaiting the need or the whim of millions of writers and speakers, always serving, always dependable, always orderly. They do so even though they find themselves tumbled into multitudes of words with multitudes of arrangements of letters. And such is their modesty and helpfulness that they submit even to the indignity of appearing in profane or unkind words. Thus, though we seldom acknowledge its stability or helpfulness, our alphabet modestly serves as our constant friend and tool.

A person can hardly contemplate our beloved letters without making observations about their appearance, their sounds, and their own odd realms of delight or discomfort. Since they are exceedingly aged but never aging, their histories fascinate us, as well. All of that induces one to imagine the alphabet as a congregation of unique and eccentric individuals—intriguing, admirable, pathetic, loveable, and, of course, frolicsome. Here they come.

Sedate and stable

The letter A, the ancient alpha,
like fragrant hay or fresh alfalfa,
provides us chewy food for thought
whenever, by some impulse caught,
we ruminate until we're sleepy
upon its pyramidal tepee.

As on the pointed A we feast,
our minds turn toward the ancient east—
to A's Egyptian forebear, *mer*,[1]
an A-shaped thing that seems to veer
off balance, leaning to the left,
much like a tippler quite bereft
of equilibrium or grace
or like a tepee tipped in space—

and then we take delight in A,
sedate and stable, built to stay.

1. Mer: the name of the Egyptian hieroglyphic symbol for pyramid.

Stand back.

Two bulges make the buxom B,
whose form is not precisely wee.
About the middle it is girt,
and so it looks both stout and pert.
If you look steadfastly at B,
you find a strange anomaly:
it seems as if its lips are pursed
and that it needs to belch or burst.

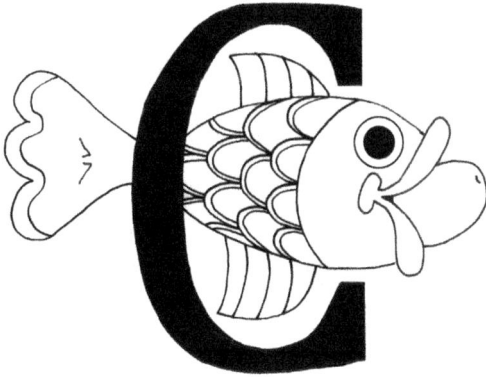

Stalker of letters

The *C* exists with mouth agape,
like fish that try to gulp a grape.
Poor *C* is lonesome, so it prowls
for consonants and tranquil vowels,
who must abandon dreamy leisure
if they should hope to elude *C*eisure.

Letter most *devious*

The letter D is undeniably most *de*vious.
It slyly lures the neophyte to rhyme *mischievious*,
an error which, indeed, would be profoundly grievious.

Letter most uncommonly common

The letter E is not a snob;
it mingles with the common mob
of letters more than any others.
At times its varied sounds it smothers,
but mute or short or pinched or long,
it's always present in the throng.
With puffy, lippy B's and P's,
or with explosive D's and T's,
or clutching C's and grasping G's,
it gives us lovely words like these:

> greasy diesels,
> sleazy weasels,
> better debtors,
> setter petters,
> Caesar's tweezers,
> wheezing geezers,
> wee malfeasance,
> flea indecence—

and flocks and herds
of far more words
that please our ears,
or tease out tears,
or squeeze a laugh
from verbal chaff.

Now, should your muse just fly on by,
should insight come in short supply,
or should vexation come to tease
your quiet mind and cause upset,
be calm: your faithful alphabet
will never cease to give you *ease*.

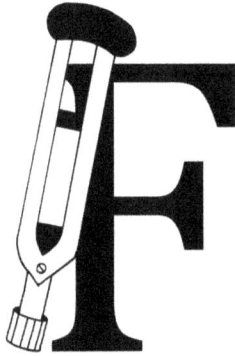

Amputee

The letter F resembles E,
which should be plain enough to see.
Now, somehow F has lost E's bottom
and craves two legs but hasn't got 'em.
Yet F, though not at all athletic,
grows neither daunted nor pathetic.
Instead, F stands quite straight and right,
(though struggling with overbite)
and, with assistance from the E,
makes *efforts* efficaciously.

Grr!

G has a sort of gulping look;
it seems about to growl,
and, like its crescent cousin C,
seems grasping for a vowel.

Choice consonants G craves, as well,
when it goes on its prowls;
for them sometimes it lingers long,
as cats lurk long for fowls.

So when the alphabet takes ease
in lounges and in bars
(in knots of letters, A's through Z's,
to smoke their rich cigars),
sly G will steal up through the haze
and grasp the nearest R's.

H is for Hellen, launcher of ships.

Endowed with overwhelming funds of common sense,
the ancient Greeks ordained the H to stand for *fence.*

So they erected H, and long it stood in Hellas:
a present, garnered from some old Phoenician fellas.

With double posts and triple bars H held its ground,
and, as time passed, the Greeks endowed mute H with sound.

Perhaps to rhyme with *beta,* then, they called it *eta.*
(But that's a guess, for scant is *eta*-rhyming data.)

Now H resembles football goals and treasures silence;
and, rising—or aspiring—over noise and violence,

exists with breathy wisps and hushed half-hisses,
quite thin and delicate, like quick Hellenic[2] kisses.

2. Being preoccupied with military arrangements in Troy, Paris probably had little time for labial exercise, even with the lips—and face—that launched the thousand Greek ships. So, in this context *Hellenic* suggests Greek kisses descending from the Platonic strain.

Letter most ego-stricken

The tiny *i* some charm affords
as grandchild of iota.
It lurks in syllables—and words
as long as Minnesota,

or, putting on its upper case
(more tall, then, and more burly),
it stands with seeming pride of place
but must feel lonesome, surely.

Yet, standing tall, it's not annoyed
by thoughts of jot or tittle,
but, as it thinks on Mr. Freud,
its torso swells a little.

Letter most sedentary

Like agile X and sleepy Z,
J shows itself infrequently,
in part because, reserved, demure,
poor J is sweetly insecure.
Let's just be frank: some people gape
at J's quite sleek and graceful shape
and then compare it to a hook,
or homely, homemade shepherd's crook,
or cane for astronaut or clown
who might try walking upside down.
But J will never take a walk
(the very thought will make it balk),
for every step poor J might take
would cause it certainly to break
both local ordinance and clause
which constitute J-walking laws.

K

Cupid's choice for the 14th

Our instinct is to pity wounded K
(which looks as if an arrow struck its side)
and wish it to be plumb and straight like H.
But straight as H may be, it lacks K's stride
as down the avenue of time K strolls,
unruffled and unchanged. Indeed, no sling
nor arrow fortune owns has hindered K,
for K has strolled through eons like a King—
with tidy waist and easy gait, perhaps
the least-changed letter of the phonic group.
In youth a hieroglyph for *palm* or *hand,*
K likely stirred the Pharaoh's crock of soup—
fresh, steaming crocodile from nearby Nile.
In truth, K's arrow wound was Cupid's work,
for though K's sound is hard, its heart is soft:

within its crooked form compassions lurk,
not only for competing, clutching C
but also for all wretches forced to dabble
long in pain with lettered wooden tiles
to make words spelled with K while playing Scrabble.
Should you get stuck with K and crave compassion,
its dent will say: "Love's never out of fashion."

Squarely elegant

In days gone by when streets were laid
and neighborhoods designed,
street planners made things on the square
and kept the L in mind.

These days developers of plots
for houses that they sell
prefer the curve and seem to say,
"Square corners look like L."

And so they do, for as a square
no letter can excel
the L as straight and true and right—
how elegant is L.

So, when some lowbrow, misinformed,
insists that straight is nought,
your gentle word is clear: "Dear friend,
please *el*evate your thought."

M

The lofty one

Amid the letters twenty-six,
with all their oddities and tricks,
the lofty M most stably stands
and literate respect commands.
It goes by neither Ms. nor Mister;
it's no one's brother, aunt, or sister.
And though its shoulders boldly rise,
its stately form and noble size
no clarifying hints display
of manliness nor feminence.
Addressing it, we rightly say
in solemn tones, "Your *Em*inence."

**A tribute to
the sole holder of an advanced degree**

Behold the N, next in the queue,
whose place in line is hardly new.
In Pharaohs' times N stood for snakes,
in Palestine for fish in lakes.
For centuries this modest gem
has felt the shadow of great M;
yet N conceals a rich surprise.
Despite its unassuming size,
despite the modesty it shows
(no curvy thighs, no classy clothes),
mild N holds powers that excel
the might of M, the dreams of L.

    For N turns *O*
    to *No*,
    reduces *one*
    to *None,*

and shrinks enduring *ever*
to vacant, empty *Never*.

Yet, far more potent than those three
persists N's power of Nth degree,
a power (like that of kings and queens)
lodged tightly in its ancient genes
and chromosomes—its DNA.
And so, this tribute we must pay:
a geek can multiply all week
but fail to scale the number peak
that N can climb in half that time
to heights that reach the sub-sublime.

Now, if you're seeking to extend
the truth to some degree, or end
an argument that isn't nice
but lack the facts to be precise,
or madly crave a rhyme for *tenth*,
you'll always find a friend in Nth.

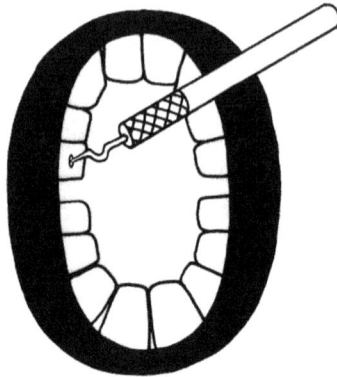

Letter most accommodating

The awful *O* of bitter anguish,
the long-drawn *O* of those who languish,
the cynic's *O*, that doubt imparts,
the *O*'s that spring from joyous hearts,
the sudden *O* when we forget,
breathe resignation or regret,
the *O* of dull preoccupation
or anger grinding with vexation,
the dentist's muted *O* repeated
(which signals that you'll be re-treated):
for all those *O*'s we owe a debt
to *O* in our own alphabet,
whose circled mouth brings oral aid
when we are troubled, pleased, afraid.

Never inclined to be peevish

In Egypt P first came to be;
in form and sense it was a mouth.
Both Greeks and Romans made it P
when Mouth migrated from the south.

The Greeks pronounced this letter *pee,*
and, for the record, so do we.
But yet, in math (one wonders why)
the self-same letter is called *pie.*

Now, P stands straight and sturdy there;
but P is just puff of air,
exploding, sweet or harsh, from lips
that kiss or utter nasty quips.

(How sad that P's can puff and purr
in peachy sweetness and allure
from that same mouth, by foulness skewed,
that hurls out P-words coarse and crude.)

Sweet P most valiantly resists
a two-leg envy that persists
when it observes quick K walk out
or stately R stroll on its route.

So, puffy P, almost sublime,
stands straight on shifting soils of time,
unlike (this *is* empirical)
old Pisa's leaning miracle.

Letter most orderly

I

In proper order stands the Q,
and quite befitting that is, too:
no matter what you think or do,
it stands before U in the queue.

II

Accepting its cue from *antique* and *unique*,
dear Q wants to alter words' ends it deems weak.
In place of drab C's and instead of dull K's,
it hopes to use *que* for effects that amaze.
Examples abound, as provided by Q;
its thoughts would grace pages, but feast on these few.

We often use *clique*—Q approves of its class
and therefore wants *chique* for a smartly-dressed lass.
And Q thinks that *meaque* is far meeker than *meek*,
and wants to persuade high-class toilets to *leaque*.

Your ugly black ink Q transforms into *inque;*
instead of just *rink,* Q now offers us *rinque;*
disdaining mere p*ink,* Q upgrades it to *pinque,*
and (far more impressive) your stink turns to *stinque.*

Now Q invites you
to join in the craze:
just drop out the K's
and drop in the *que.*

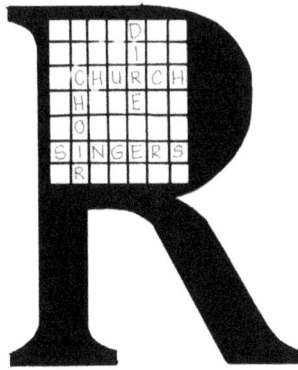

Sometimes silent in the choir

For volunteeuhs within the kwiah,
the R can pose a problem diah,
foh the directuh offuhs threats,
should singuhs mah Mozaht motets
by snahling ah's like cawtly fools,
a gross infraction of his rules.

But dear, self-conscious R feels grey
those times he hears the maestro say,
"Who's got the awful Midwest R's?"
Then, when the choir gets to their cars,
R sees them checking their behinds
and wonders what is in their minds.

Bewildered R, to get away,
strolls out to J with kingly K,
and smothers all the choral babble
with K and J in well-spelled Scrabble.

Essence of profusion—sine qua one

Both shape and sound of S suggest
to some the serpent sly, the snake,
deceiver of our mother Eve.
But let us roundly laud the S.
This graceful letter, twice-curved sign,
this suave and swan-like consonant,
holds strength no other letters own.

Without prolific, plural S
how greatly would our world regress.
Your shopping cart would hold far less,
your billfold hold just one thin bill,
prescriptions just a lonesome pill.
Your road towards home would have one lane,
your lonely auto one glass pane.
For driving you would have one eye,
one busy hand and arm, one thigh.
Once home, you'd struggle through the yard,
for walking on one leg is hard.

The only nostril in your nose
would smell the season's only rose.
Your single, single-fingered hand
could never stretch a rubber band
or tie your ties or straps or strings—
or help you with a thousand things.
But, far beyond those tiny pains,
without the S you'd have no brains.
(And that, of course, might make you cry
one hopeless tear from your one eye.)

Conceive the world's abject distress
without the multiplying S.
Life would be filled with emptiness:
no persons, animals, or trees,
no, rivers, mountains, skies, or seas,
no cities, buildings—none of these.
And one bleak ocean we would share
to sail our single vessel there—
and each with single, eager eye
would spy one star to steer it by.
So, on would go our narrow lives,
bereft of friends, and kids, and wives.
Consider well our crazy mess
without the letter we must bless—
essential, multiplying S.

Never tedious

A life-long friend to you and
me
is sturdy, steadfast, modest
T.

It's present in nativi-
T,
(when first we gain some liber-
T),

remains attached in puber-
T
(that time of odd proclivi-
T),

then lingers through minori-
T
(the years of party repar-
T),

holds firmly through majori-
T
(accepting wealth or pover-
T),

and ends our cold senili-
T
(with all its bleak fragili-
T).

Give thought to steadfast, modest
T,
that life-long friend to you and
me.

U

Letter indispensable to you

We must admire the humble U,
perpetual helper to the Q.
Without shy U, Q would be mute,
and not one baby could be *cute*.
Oh, gone would be pool *cue* and *ruby;*
and where—without U—where would *you* be?

Two for V

I

Should you of slender V request,
"Would it be good to double you?"
it might suggest that it were best
to let its shape not trouble you.
For V, a valley or a wedge,
has every happy right to be
well balanced on its bottom edge—
for that's the point of being V.

II
Roman Tea V

When Romans owned the alphabet
the double U was not there yet.
But still they loved to hear its whiff,
so when they bent to blow their tea,
they cooled it with their whiffy V.

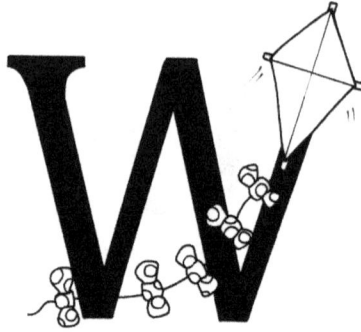

Silent maker of wind

Inverted M of sorts and wide of girth,
the chubby double U makes silent wind
for windless letters alphabetical.

So, though its lengthy name might signal worth,
its substance is but wind—and in the end
its strength is strictly theoretical.

> (And odd it is that double U
> is not a double V,
> for that is what its bumpy frame
> most clearly wants to be.)

Alphabetical acrobat

Pity ugly X:
its sound almost crude,
its frame all athwart,
it's forced to consort
(but not to collude)
with movies quite lewd.
Pity wretched X.

Envy favored X:
in life's game (or fight)
when some sudden toss
brings upside-down loss
(like dice from a height),
lithe X lands just right.
Envy agile X.

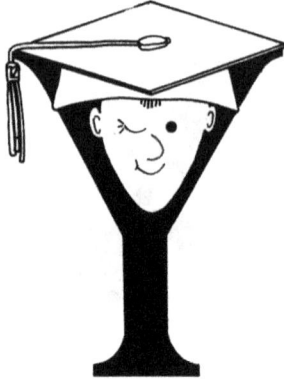

Wise guy

If on our ears
our minds rely,
we must agree
the letter Y
most surely vies
to be most wise.

Yet *wise* contains
no letter Y.
And that reveals
to our mind's eye
the guise of guys
that we *call* wise.

Oh, Zo very Zleepy

It takez zo long to reach the Z
it fallz azleep, az you can zee,
then dreamz to find itz proper place
in placez where it zhouldn't be.
It getz itzelf confuzed with S
and failz to zpell with much zuczezz.
Zo let uz not dizrupt poor Z,
but in itz dreamz this mezzage trace:
Zleepy Z, zleep eazy;
zleep eazy, zleepy Z.